50 Ultimate Game Day Snacks

By: Kelly Johnson

Table of Contents

- Buffalo Cauliflower Bites
- Guacamole with Crunchy Tortilla Chips
- Cheesy Spinach and Artichoke Dip
- Loaded Nachos
- Jalapeño Poppers
- BBQ Chicken Sliders
- Crispy Onion Rings
- Baked Buffalo Wings
- Sweet and Spicy Meatballs
- Pimento Cheese Dip
- Mini Quesadillas
- Bacon-Wrapped Jalapeños
- Veggie Platter with Hummus
- Sloppy Joe Sliders
- Homemade Potato Chips
- Stuffed Mushrooms
- Mozzarella Sticks with Marinara Sauce
- Guacamole-Stuffed Cherry Tomatoes
- Spinach and Feta Stuffed Pastry Bites
- Beef Empanadas
- Cheddar and Chive Biscuits
- Mini Taco Cups
- Sweet Potato Fries with Chipotle Mayo
- Crispy Chickpea Snack
- Honey BBQ Wings
- Loaded Potato Skins
- Veggie and Cheese Spring Rolls
- Baked Zucchini Fries
- Pulled Pork Sliders
- Hummus and Pita Chips
- Grilled Cheese Bites with Tomato Soup
- Deviled Eggs with Bacon
- Crispy Chicken Tenders with Ranch
- Nacho Cheese Dip
- Sriracha Honey Chicken Bites

- BBQ Pork Nachos
- Mini Corn Dogs
- Roasted Garlic Parmesan Popcorn
- Caprese Skewers
- Sweet Chili Chicken Wings
- Spinach and Artichoke Stuffed Bread
- Pulled Chicken Queso Dip
- Baked Mozzarella Sticks
- Roasted Beet and Goat Cheese Crostini
- Classic Sliders with Cheese
- Coconut Shrimp with Sweet Chili Sauce
- Bacon-Wrapped Potato Bites
- Baked Sweet Potato Nachos
- Jalapeño Cheddar Cornbread Muffins
- Mini Chicken and Waffle Bites

Buffalo Cauliflower Bites

Ingredients:

- 1 head of cauliflower, cut into florets
- 1 cup all-purpose flour
- 1/2 cup almond milk
- 1/2 cup breadcrumbs
- 1 cup buffalo sauce
- 1 tbsp olive oil
- Salt and pepper to taste
- Fresh parsley for garnish

Instructions:

1. Preheat your oven to 400°F (200°C). Line a baking sheet with parchment paper.
2. In a bowl, mix the flour, almond milk, salt, and pepper to create a batter.
3. Dip each cauliflower floret into the batter, then roll it in breadcrumbs. Place on the baking sheet.
4. Drizzle olive oil over the cauliflower and bake for 20-25 minutes, until crispy and golden.
5. Toss the baked cauliflower in buffalo sauce and return to the oven for another 5 minutes.
6. Garnish with fresh parsley and serve hot.

Guacamole with Crunchy Tortilla Chips

Ingredients:

- 3 ripe avocados, mashed
- 1 small onion, finely chopped
- 1 tomato, diced
- 1 lime, juiced
- 1/2 tsp cumin
- Salt and pepper to taste
- Tortilla chips for dipping

Instructions:

1. In a bowl, combine the mashed avocados, onion, tomato, lime juice, cumin, salt, and pepper. Mix well.
2. Serve immediately with crunchy tortilla chips for dipping. Enjoy as a fresh and creamy appetizer!

Cheesy Spinach and Artichoke Dip

Ingredients:

- 1 cup frozen spinach, thawed and drained
- 1 cup canned artichoke hearts, chopped
- 1/2 cup cream cheese
- 1/2 cup sour cream
- 1 cup shredded mozzarella cheese
- 1/2 cup grated Parmesan cheese
- 2 garlic cloves, minced
- Salt and pepper to taste

Instructions:

1. Preheat the oven to 375°F (190°C). Grease a baking dish.
2. In a bowl, combine the spinach, artichokes, cream cheese, sour cream, mozzarella, Parmesan, and garlic. Stir until smooth.
3. Season with salt and pepper and transfer to the prepared baking dish.
4. Bake for 20-25 minutes until the top is golden and bubbly.
5. Serve warm with crackers or bread for dipping.

Loaded Nachos

Ingredients:

- 1 bag tortilla chips
- 1 cup shredded cheddar cheese
- 1 cup black beans, drained and rinsed
- 1/2 cup diced tomatoes
- 1/4 cup sliced jalapeños
- 1/2 cup guacamole
- 1/4 cup sour cream
- Salsa for serving

Instructions:

1. Preheat your oven to 375°F (190°C).
2. Arrange the tortilla chips in a single layer on a baking sheet. Top with cheese, black beans, tomatoes, and jalapeños.
3. Bake for 10-12 minutes, until the cheese is melted and bubbly.
4. Serve with guacamole, sour cream, and salsa on the side for dipping.

Jalapeño Poppers

Ingredients:

- 12 fresh jalapeños, halved and seeds removed
- 1 package cream cheese, softened
- 1/2 cup shredded cheddar cheese
- 1/4 cup cooked bacon, crumbled (optional)
- 1/2 cup breadcrumbs
- 1 tbsp olive oil

Instructions:

1. Preheat the oven to 375°F (190°C). Line a baking sheet with parchment paper.
2. Mix the cream cheese, cheddar cheese, and bacon in a bowl.
3. Stuff each jalapeño half with the cheese mixture and place on the baking sheet.
4. Sprinkle breadcrumbs on top of each stuffed jalapeño and drizzle with olive oil.
5. Bake for 15-20 minutes, until golden and crispy.

BBQ Chicken Sliders

Ingredients:

- 2 cups cooked chicken, shredded
- 1/2 cup BBQ sauce
- 12 slider buns
- 1/4 cup pickles, sliced
- 1/4 cup coleslaw (optional)

Instructions:

1. In a bowl, combine the shredded chicken and BBQ sauce. Stir to coat.
2. Toast the slider buns in the oven or on a griddle.
3. Assemble the sliders by placing a spoonful of BBQ chicken on the bottom half of each bun.
4. Top with pickles and coleslaw, then place the top bun on. Serve immediately.

Crispy Onion Rings

Ingredients:

- 2 large onions, sliced into rings
- 1 cup flour
- 1 cup breadcrumbs
- 1/2 tsp paprika
- 1/2 tsp garlic powder
- 1/2 cup almond milk
- Salt and pepper to taste
- Vegetable oil for frying

Instructions:

1. Heat vegetable oil in a deep fryer or large pan to 350°F (175°C).
2. In a bowl, mix the flour, breadcrumbs, paprika, garlic powder, salt, and pepper.
3. Dip the onion rings in almond milk, then coat with the breadcrumb mixture.
4. Fry the onion rings in batches for 2-3 minutes, until golden and crispy.
5. Drain on paper towels and serve hot with dipping sauce.

Baked Buffalo Wings

Ingredients:

- 12 chicken wings
- 1/4 cup olive oil
- 1/4 cup buffalo sauce
- 1 tbsp garlic powder
- 1 tbsp onion powder
- Salt and pepper to taste

Instructions:

1. Preheat the oven to 400°F (200°C). Line a baking sheet with parchment paper.
2. Toss the chicken wings in olive oil, buffalo sauce, garlic powder, onion powder, salt, and pepper.
3. Arrange the wings in a single layer on the baking sheet.
4. Bake for 25-30 minutes, flipping halfway through, until crispy and cooked through.
5. Serve with ranch or blue cheese dressing on the side.

Sweet and Spicy Meatballs

Ingredients:

- 1 lb ground beef or turkey
- 1/4 cup breadcrumbs
- 1 egg
- 2 tbsp soy sauce
- 2 tbsp honey
- 1 tbsp sriracha sauce
- 1 tbsp olive oil
- 1 garlic clove, minced
- Salt and pepper to taste

Instructions:

1. Preheat the oven to 375°F (190°C). Line a baking sheet with parchment paper.
2. In a bowl, mix the ground meat, breadcrumbs, egg, soy sauce, salt, and pepper. Form into small meatballs and place on the baking sheet.
3. Bake for 15-20 minutes, until browned and cooked through.
4. In a small saucepan, heat the honey, sriracha, and garlic over medium heat. Stir to combine.
5. Toss the cooked meatballs in the sweet and spicy sauce and serve warm.

Pimento Cheese Dip

Ingredients:

- 1 cup shredded sharp cheddar cheese
- 1/2 cup cream cheese, softened
- 1/4 cup mayonnaise
- 2 tbsp pimentos, chopped
- 1 tbsp Dijon mustard
- 1/2 tsp garlic powder
- Salt and pepper to taste
- Fresh parsley for garnish

Instructions:

1. In a bowl, combine the shredded cheddar, cream cheese, mayonnaise, pimentos, mustard, garlic powder, salt, and pepper.
2. Mix until smooth and creamy.
3. Garnish with fresh parsley and serve with crackers or veggies.

Mini Quesadillas

Ingredients:

- 4 small flour tortillas
- 1 cup shredded cheese (cheddar, Monterey Jack, or a blend)
- 1/2 cup cooked chicken or beef (optional)
- 1/4 cup diced onions
- 1/4 cup diced bell peppers
- Salsa and sour cream for dipping

Instructions:

1. Heat a skillet over medium heat.
2. Place a tortilla in the skillet and sprinkle with cheese, cooked chicken or beef, onions, and peppers.
3. Top with another tortilla and cook for 2-3 minutes per side until golden brown and the cheese has melted.
4. Remove from heat and cut into small wedges. Serve with salsa and sour cream.

Bacon-Wrapped Jalapeños

Ingredients:

- 10 fresh jalapeños, halved and seeds removed
- 1/2 cup cream cheese
- 1/2 cup shredded cheddar cheese
- 10 slices of bacon
- Toothpicks for securing

Instructions:

1. Preheat the oven to 375°F (190°C). Line a baking sheet with parchment paper.
2. In a bowl, mix the cream cheese and cheddar cheese.
3. Stuff each jalapeño half with the cheese mixture.
4. Wrap each stuffed jalapeño with a slice of bacon and secure with a toothpick.
5. Bake for 20-25 minutes, until the bacon is crispy. Serve hot.

Veggie Platter with Hummus

Ingredients:

- 1 cucumber, sliced
- 1 bell pepper, sliced
- 1 cup cherry tomatoes
- 1 cup baby carrots
- 1/2 cup celery, cut into sticks
- 1 cup hummus (store-bought or homemade)

Instructions:

1. Arrange the sliced veggies (cucumber, bell pepper, tomatoes, carrots, and celery) on a large platter.
2. Place a bowl of hummus in the center for dipping.
3. Serve as a fresh and healthy appetizer.

Sloppy Joe Sliders

Ingredients:

- 1 lb ground beef or turkey
- 1/2 onion, diced
- 1 cup sloppy joe sauce (store-bought or homemade)
- 12 slider buns
- 1/2 cup shredded cheese (optional)

Instructions:

1. In a skillet, cook the ground beef or turkey with the diced onion over medium heat until browned.
2. Add the sloppy joe sauce and simmer for 5-10 minutes until thickened.
3. Spoon the sloppy joe mixture onto slider buns, top with shredded cheese (if using), and serve immediately.

Homemade Potato Chips

Ingredients:

- 4 large potatoes, thinly sliced
- 2 tbsp olive oil
- Salt to taste
- Fresh herbs (optional, for garnish)

Instructions:

1. Preheat the oven to 400°F (200°C). Line a baking sheet with parchment paper.
2. Toss the potato slices in olive oil and season with salt.
3. Spread the potatoes in a single layer on the baking sheet.
4. Bake for 15-20 minutes, flipping halfway through, until crispy and golden brown.
5. Garnish with fresh herbs (optional) and serve.

Stuffed Mushrooms

Ingredients:

- 12 large mushrooms, stems removed
- 4 oz cream cheese, softened
- 1/4 cup grated Parmesan cheese
- 1/4 cup breadcrumbs
- 2 tbsp garlic, minced
- Salt and pepper to taste
- Fresh parsley for garnish

Instructions:

1. Preheat the oven to 375°F (190°C). Line a baking sheet with parchment paper.
2. In a bowl, mix the cream cheese, Parmesan cheese, breadcrumbs, garlic, salt, and pepper.
3. Stuff each mushroom cap with the cream cheese mixture and place on the baking sheet.
4. Bake for 20 minutes, until the mushrooms are tender and the tops are golden brown.
5. Garnish with fresh parsley and serve.

Mozzarella Sticks with Marinara Sauce

Ingredients:

- 12 mozzarella string cheese sticks, cut in half
- 1 cup breadcrumbs
- 1/2 cup all-purpose flour
- 2 eggs, beaten
- 1 tsp garlic powder
- 1 tsp dried oregano
- 1 cup marinara sauce

Instructions:

1. Preheat the oven to 400°F (200°C). Line a baking sheet with parchment paper.
2. In a shallow dish, mix the breadcrumbs, garlic powder, and oregano.
3. Dip each mozzarella stick in flour, then egg, and then coat with the breadcrumb mixture.
4. Arrange the mozzarella sticks on the baking sheet and bake for 10-12 minutes, until golden and crispy.
5. Serve with marinara sauce for dipping.

Guacamole-Stuffed Cherry Tomatoes

Ingredients:

- 12 cherry tomatoes, halved
- 1 ripe avocado, mashed
- 1/4 cup red onion, finely chopped
- 1 tbsp cilantro, chopped
- 1 tbsp lime juice
- Salt and pepper to taste

Instructions:

1. Hollow out each cherry tomato half and set aside.
2. In a bowl, mix the mashed avocado, red onion, cilantro, lime juice, salt, and pepper.
3. Spoon the guacamole mixture into each tomato half and serve immediately.

Spinach and Feta Stuffed Pastry Bites

Ingredients:

- 1 sheet puff pastry
- 2 cups fresh spinach, chopped
- 1/2 cup feta cheese, crumbled
- 1/4 cup ricotta cheese
- 1/4 tsp garlic powder
- 1/4 tsp nutmeg
- 1 egg (for egg wash)
- Salt and pepper to taste

Instructions:

1. Preheat the oven to 375°F (190°C). Line a baking sheet with parchment paper.
2. In a pan, sauté the spinach until wilted, then drain excess moisture.
3. In a bowl, mix the spinach, feta, ricotta, garlic powder, nutmeg, salt, and pepper.
4. Roll out the puff pastry and cut into squares.
5. Place a spoonful of the spinach mixture in the center of each square.
6. Fold the pastry into a triangle or square, sealing the edges.
7. Brush with egg wash and bake for 15-20 minutes, until golden and puffed.

Beef Empanadas

Ingredients:

- 1 lb ground beef
- 1/2 onion, chopped
- 1/4 cup green olives, chopped
- 1/4 cup raisins
- 1 tsp cumin
- 1 tsp paprika
- 1/2 tsp chili powder
- 1/2 cup beef broth
- 1 package empanada dough or pie crust
- 1 egg (for egg wash)

Instructions:

1. In a skillet, cook the ground beef with onions until browned.
2. Stir in the olives, raisins, cumin, paprika, chili powder, and beef broth. Simmer until thickened.
3. Roll out the empanada dough and cut into circles.
4. Place a spoonful of the beef mixture in the center of each dough circle.
5. Fold the dough over and press the edges to seal.
6. Brush with egg wash and bake at 375°F (190°C) for 20-25 minutes, until golden.

Cheddar and Chive Biscuits

Ingredients:

- 2 cups all-purpose flour
- 2 tsp baking powder
- 1/2 tsp salt
- 1/4 tsp baking soda
- 1/2 cup cold butter, cubed
- 1 cup sharp cheddar cheese, shredded
- 2 tbsp fresh chives, chopped
- 3/4 cup buttermilk

Instructions:

1. Preheat the oven to 400°F (200°C). Line a baking sheet with parchment paper.
2. In a bowl, whisk together the flour, baking powder, salt, and baking soda.
3. Cut in the cold butter until the mixture resembles coarse crumbs.
4. Stir in the cheese, chives, and buttermilk until just combined.
5. Drop spoonfuls of dough onto the baking sheet and bake for 12-15 minutes, until golden.

Mini Taco Cups

Ingredients:

- 1 lb ground beef or chicken
- 1 packet taco seasoning
- 1/2 cup water
- 12 mini tortilla cups (store-bought or homemade)
- 1 cup shredded cheddar cheese
- 1/2 cup sour cream
- Salsa and jalapeños for garnish

Instructions:

1. Cook the ground meat in a skillet and add taco seasoning and water. Simmer until thickened.
2. Spoon the taco mixture into the mini tortilla cups.
3. Top with shredded cheese and bake at 350°F (175°C) for 5-7 minutes, until the cheese is melted.
4. Garnish with sour cream, salsa, and jalapeños.

Sweet Potato Fries with Chipotle Mayo

Ingredients:

- 2 large sweet potatoes, cut into fries
- 2 tbsp olive oil
- 1/2 tsp paprika
- Salt and pepper to taste
- 1/2 cup mayonnaise
- 1 tbsp chipotle in adobo sauce, minced
- 1 tsp lime juice

Instructions:

1. Preheat the oven to 400°F (200°C). Line a baking sheet with parchment paper.
2. Toss the sweet potato fries in olive oil, paprika, salt, and pepper.
3. Spread the fries in a single layer and bake for 25-30 minutes, flipping halfway through.
4. In a small bowl, mix mayonnaise, chipotle, and lime juice to make the dip.
5. Serve the fries with the chipotle mayo.

Crispy Chickpea Snack

Ingredients:

- 1 can chickpeas, drained and rinsed
- 1 tbsp olive oil
- 1/2 tsp paprika
- 1/4 tsp cumin
- Salt to taste

Instructions:

1. Preheat the oven to 400°F (200°C). Line a baking sheet with parchment paper.
2. Toss the chickpeas with olive oil, paprika, cumin, and salt.
3. Spread the chickpeas in a single layer on the baking sheet.
4. Bake for 25-30 minutes, shaking the pan halfway through, until crispy.
5. Let cool and serve as a crunchy snack.

Honey BBQ Wings

Ingredients:

- 10 chicken wings
- 1/4 cup honey
- 1/4 cup BBQ sauce
- 1 tbsp olive oil
- 1 tsp garlic powder
- Salt and pepper to taste

Instructions:

1. Preheat the oven to 400°F (200°C). Line a baking sheet with parchment paper.
2. Toss the wings in olive oil, garlic powder, salt, and pepper.
3. Arrange the wings on the baking sheet and bake for 25-30 minutes until crispy.
4. In a bowl, mix honey and BBQ sauce. Toss the cooked wings in the sauce and serve.

Loaded Potato Skins

Ingredients:

- 4 large russet potatoes, baked and halved
- 1 cup shredded cheddar cheese
- 1/4 cup sour cream
- 1/4 cup cooked bacon, crumbled
- 2 tbsp green onions, chopped
- Salt and pepper to taste

Instructions:

1. Preheat the oven to 375°F (190°C).
2. Scoop out the flesh from the baked potato halves, leaving a thin layer of potato.
3. Place the potato skins on a baking sheet and bake for 10 minutes until crispy.
4. Fill the potato skins with cheese, bacon, and a sprinkle of salt and pepper.
5. Bake for another 10 minutes until the cheese melts.
6. Top with sour cream and green onions before serving.

Veggie and Cheese Spring Rolls

Ingredients:

- 8 rice paper wrappers
- 1 cup mixed veggies (carrots, cucumbers, bell peppers, etc.), julienned
- 1/2 cup shredded cheese (cheddar, mozzarella, or your choice)
- 2 tbsp fresh cilantro, chopped
- Sweet chili sauce for dipping

Instructions:

1. Soak the rice paper wrappers in warm water for 10-15 seconds, then lay them flat on a clean surface.
2. Layer the veggies, cheese, and cilantro in the center of each wrapper.
3. Fold in the sides and roll tightly to form a spring roll.
4. Serve with sweet chili sauce for dipping.

Baked Zucchini Fries

Ingredients:

- 2 medium zucchinis, sliced into fries
- 1/2 cup breadcrumbs
- 1/4 cup grated Parmesan cheese
- 1/2 tsp garlic powder
- 1/2 tsp paprika
- Salt and pepper to taste
- 1 egg, beaten

Instructions:

1. Preheat the oven to 400°F (200°C). Line a baking sheet with parchment paper.
2. In a shallow bowl, mix breadcrumbs, Parmesan, garlic powder, paprika, salt, and pepper.
3. Dip each zucchini slice into the egg, then coat with the breadcrumb mixture.
4. Arrange the coated zucchini fries in a single layer on the baking sheet.
5. Bake for 20-25 minutes, flipping halfway through, until crispy and golden.
6. Serve with marinara or ranch sauce for dipping.

Pulled Pork Sliders

Ingredients:

- 2 cups pulled pork (cooked)
- 8 slider buns
- 1/2 cup coleslaw
- 1/4 cup BBQ sauce
- Pickles (optional)

Instructions:

1. Preheat the oven to 350°F (175°C).
2. Warm the pulled pork and mix with BBQ sauce.
3. Split the slider buns and place the bottom halves on a baking sheet.
4. Layer the pulled pork on each bun and top with coleslaw.
5. Add pickles if desired, then place the top buns on.
6. Bake for 5-7 minutes, until the buns are slightly toasted.
7. Serve warm.

Hummus and Pita Chips

Ingredients:

- 1 cup hummus (store-bought or homemade)
- 4 pita breads, cut into triangles
- Olive oil for brushing
- 1/2 tsp paprika (optional)
- Salt to taste

Instructions:

1. Preheat the oven to 400°F (200°C).
2. Arrange pita triangles on a baking sheet and brush with olive oil.
3. Sprinkle with paprika and salt.
4. Bake for 8-10 minutes, until crispy and golden.
5. Serve with hummus for dipping.

Grilled Cheese Bites with Tomato Soup

Ingredients:

- 4 slices of bread
- 4 slices of cheese (cheddar, American, or your favorite)
- 1 tbsp butter
- 1 cup tomato soup (for dipping)

Instructions:

1. Butter one side of each slice of bread.
2. Place a slice of cheese between two pieces of bread, buttered sides out.
3. Grill the sandwich in a skillet over medium heat until golden brown on both sides and the cheese is melted.
4. Cut the grilled cheese into bite-sized squares.
5. Serve with warm tomato soup for dipping.

Deviled Eggs with Bacon

Ingredients:

- 6 hard-boiled eggs, peeled and halved
- 1/4 cup mayonnaise
- 1 tsp Dijon mustard
- 1 tsp white vinegar
- Salt and pepper to taste
- 2 slices bacon, cooked and crumbled
- Paprika for garnish

Instructions:

1. Remove the yolks from the boiled egg halves and mash them in a bowl.
2. Mix in mayonnaise, mustard, vinegar, salt, and pepper.
3. Spoon or pipe the filling back into the egg whites.
4. Top with crumbled bacon and a sprinkle of paprika.
5. Serve chilled.

Crispy Chicken Tenders with Ranch

Ingredients:

- 1 lb chicken tenders
- 1 cup breadcrumbs
- 1/2 cup flour
- 1 egg, beaten
- 1/2 tsp garlic powder
- 1/2 tsp paprika
- Salt and pepper to taste
- 1 cup ranch dressing for dipping

Instructions:

1. Preheat the oven to 400°F (200°C). Line a baking sheet with parchment paper.
2. Season the flour with garlic powder, paprika, salt, and pepper.
3. Dredge each chicken tender in the flour, then dip in the egg, and coat with breadcrumbs.
4. Arrange the tenders on the baking sheet and bake for 20-25 minutes, flipping halfway through, until crispy.
5. Serve with ranch dressing for dipping.

Nacho Cheese Dip

Ingredients:

- 1 cup shredded cheddar cheese
- 1/2 cup cream cheese
- 1/4 cup sour cream
- 1/4 cup milk
- 1/2 tsp garlic powder
- 1/2 tsp onion powder
- 1/2 tsp chili powder
- Salt and pepper to taste

Instructions:

1. In a saucepan, melt the cream cheese over medium heat.
2. Stir in the sour cream, milk, and spices.
3. Gradually add the cheddar cheese, stirring until melted and smooth.
4. Serve warm with tortilla chips or veggies for dipping.

Sriracha Honey Chicken Bites

Ingredients:

- 1 lb chicken breast, cut into bite-sized cubes
- 1/4 cup Sriracha sauce
- 2 tbsp honey
- 1 tbsp soy sauce
- 1 tbsp olive oil
- 1/4 tsp garlic powder
- Sesame seeds for garnish (optional)

Instructions:

1. Heat olive oil in a skillet over medium heat. Add chicken and cook until golden and cooked through, about 6-8 minutes.
2. In a bowl, mix together Sriracha, honey, soy sauce, and garlic powder.
3. Pour the sauce over the cooked chicken and toss to coat.
4. Cook for an additional 2-3 minutes, until the sauce thickens.
5. Garnish with sesame seeds and serve warm.

BBQ Pork Nachos

Ingredients:

- 2 cups pulled pork (cooked)
- 1 bag tortilla chips
- 1 cup shredded cheddar cheese
- 1/2 cup BBQ sauce
- 1/4 cup sliced jalapeños
- 1/4 cup sour cream
- 1/4 cup chopped green onions

Instructions:

1. Preheat the oven to 375°F (190°C). Line a baking sheet with parchment paper.
2. Spread tortilla chips evenly on the baking sheet.
3. Layer the pulled pork on top of the chips, followed by cheese and jalapeños.
4. Drizzle with BBQ sauce and bake for 10-12 minutes, until the cheese is melted and bubbly.
5. Top with sour cream and green onions before serving.

Mini Corn Dogs

Ingredients:

- 12 mini hot dogs
- 1 cup cornmeal
- 1/2 cup flour
- 1 tsp baking powder
- 1/2 tsp salt
- 1/2 tsp paprika
- 1/2 cup buttermilk
- 1 egg
- Vegetable oil for frying
- Mustard or ketchup for dipping

Instructions:

1. Heat the oil in a deep fryer or large pot to 375°F (190°C).
2. In a bowl, mix cornmeal, flour, baking powder, salt, and paprika.
3. Whisk in buttermilk and egg until smooth.
4. Insert toothpicks into the mini hot dogs and dip them into the batter.
5. Fry in batches for 2-3 minutes until golden and crispy.
6. Drain on paper towels and serve with mustard or ketchup.

Roasted Garlic Parmesan Popcorn

Ingredients:

- 1/2 cup popcorn kernels
- 2 tbsp olive oil
- 3 cloves garlic, minced
- 1/4 cup grated Parmesan cheese
- Salt and pepper to taste
- 1 tbsp chopped fresh parsley (optional)

Instructions:

1. Pop the popcorn kernels using your preferred method.
2. In a small pan, heat olive oil over medium heat. Add garlic and cook for 1-2 minutes until fragrant.
3. Pour the garlic-infused oil over the popped popcorn and toss to coat.
4. Sprinkle Parmesan cheese, salt, and pepper over the popcorn and toss again.
5. Garnish with fresh parsley if desired and serve.

Caprese Skewers

Ingredients:

- 1 pint cherry tomatoes
- 1/2 lb fresh mozzarella balls (bocconcini or ciliegine)
- Fresh basil leaves
- Balsamic glaze for drizzling
- Salt and pepper to taste

Instructions:

1. Thread a cherry tomato, a basil leaf, and a mozzarella ball onto each skewer.
2. Repeat until all ingredients are used.
3. Drizzle with balsamic glaze and season with salt and pepper.
4. Serve immediately or refrigerate until ready to serve.

Sweet Chili Chicken Wings

Ingredients:

- 12 chicken wings
- 1/4 cup sweet chili sauce
- 1 tbsp soy sauce
- 1 tbsp rice vinegar
- 1/2 tsp garlic powder
- 1 tbsp sesame seeds (optional)
- Fresh cilantro for garnish (optional)

Instructions:

1. Preheat the oven to 400°F (200°C). Line a baking sheet with parchment paper.
2. Toss the chicken wings with garlic powder, then bake for 25-30 minutes, flipping halfway through, until crispy.
3. In a small bowl, mix sweet chili sauce, soy sauce, and rice vinegar.
4. Once the wings are done, toss them in the sauce mixture.
5. Garnish with sesame seeds and fresh cilantro before serving.

Spinach and Artichoke Stuffed Bread

Ingredients:

- 1 loaf French bread or baguette
- 1 cup cooked spinach, drained
- 1/2 cup canned artichoke hearts, chopped
- 1/2 cup cream cheese, softened
- 1/4 cup mayonnaise
- 1/2 cup grated Parmesan cheese
- 1/2 cup shredded mozzarella cheese
- 1 tbsp garlic, minced
- Salt and pepper to taste

Instructions:

1. Preheat the oven to 375°F (190°C). Cut the loaf of bread into halves or quarters, depending on size.
2. In a bowl, combine spinach, artichokes, cream cheese, mayonnaise, Parmesan, mozzarella, garlic, salt, and pepper.
3. Hollow out the bread and stuff the cavity with the spinach-artichoke mixture.
4. Wrap the stuffed bread in foil and bake for 15-20 minutes.
5. Unwrap the foil and bake for an additional 5-7 minutes, until the top is golden and bubbly.
6. Serve warm.

Pulled Chicken Queso Dip

Ingredients:

- 2 cups cooked shredded chicken
- 1 cup cheddar cheese, shredded
- 1 cup cream cheese, softened
- 1/2 cup salsa
- 1/2 cup sour cream
- 1/2 tsp chili powder
- 1/4 tsp cumin
- Salt to taste
- Tortilla chips for serving

Instructions:

1. In a medium saucepan, combine all ingredients over medium heat.
2. Stir until the cheese has melted and the dip is smooth.
3. Season with chili powder, cumin, and salt.
4. Serve warm with tortilla chips.

Baked Mozzarella Sticks

Ingredients:

- 12 mozzarella cheese sticks
- 1/2 cup flour
- 1/2 cup breadcrumbs
- 1/2 tsp garlic powder
- 1/2 tsp Italian seasoning
- 1 egg, beaten
- Salt and pepper to taste
- Marinara sauce for dipping

Instructions:

1. Preheat the oven to 400°F (200°C). Line a baking sheet with parchment paper.
2. In a shallow bowl, mix flour, breadcrumbs, garlic powder, Italian seasoning, salt, and pepper.
3. Dip each mozzarella stick into the flour mixture, then into the egg, and back into the flour mixture.
4. Arrange the coated mozzarella sticks on the baking sheet and bake for 8-10 minutes until golden and crispy.
5. Serve with marinara sauce for dipping.

Roasted Beet and Goat Cheese Crostini

Ingredients:

- 1 loaf baguette, sliced into 1/2-inch pieces
- 2 medium beets, roasted and peeled, sliced thinly
- 4 oz goat cheese, softened
- 2 tbsp olive oil
- 1 tsp fresh thyme leaves
- Salt and pepper to taste

Instructions:

1. Preheat the oven to 375°F (190°C). Arrange baguette slices on a baking sheet and brush with olive oil.
2. Toast the bread for 5-7 minutes, until golden.
3. Spread goat cheese on each crostini.
4. Top with beet slices, a sprinkle of fresh thyme, salt, and pepper.
5. Serve immediately.

Classic Sliders with Cheese

Ingredients:

- 1 lb ground beef
- 8 small slider buns
- 8 slices cheddar cheese
- 1 tbsp olive oil
- 1/2 tsp garlic powder
- Salt and pepper to taste
- Pickles and ketchup for serving

Instructions:

1. Form the ground beef into 8 small patties and season with garlic powder, salt, and pepper.
2. Heat olive oil in a skillet over medium heat. Cook the patties for 3-4 minutes per side, or until desired doneness.
3. Place a slice of cheese on each patty during the last minute of cooking to melt.
4. Assemble the sliders on the buns with pickles and ketchup.
5. Serve warm.

Coconut Shrimp with Sweet Chili Sauce

Ingredients:

- 1 lb large shrimp, peeled and deveined
- 1/2 cup all-purpose flour
- 2 large eggs, beaten
- 1 cup shredded coconut
- 1/2 cup panko breadcrumbs
- Salt and pepper to taste
- Vegetable oil for frying
- 1/2 cup sweet chili sauce for dipping

Instructions:

1. Preheat the oil in a deep fryer or large pot to 375°F (190°C).
2. Season the shrimp with salt and pepper. Dredge each shrimp in flour, dip in beaten egg, then coat with a mixture of shredded coconut and panko breadcrumbs.
3. Fry the shrimp in batches for 2-3 minutes, or until golden brown and crispy.
4. Drain on paper towels. Serve with sweet chili sauce for dipping.

Bacon-Wrapped Potato Bites

Ingredients:

- 12 small baby potatoes, halved
- 12 slices bacon
- 1/4 cup olive oil
- 1 tsp garlic powder
- 1 tsp smoked paprika
- Salt and pepper to taste
- Fresh chives for garnish (optional)

Instructions:

1. Preheat the oven to 400°F (200°C). Line a baking sheet with parchment paper.
2. Toss the potato halves in olive oil, garlic powder, paprika, salt, and pepper.
3. Wrap each potato half with a slice of bacon, securing with toothpicks if necessary.
4. Arrange the bacon-wrapped potatoes on the baking sheet and bake for 25-30 minutes, or until the bacon is crispy and the potatoes are tender.
5. Garnish with fresh chives before serving.

Baked Sweet Potato Nachos

Ingredients:

- 2 medium sweet potatoes, peeled and cut into thin rounds
- 1 tbsp olive oil
- Salt and pepper to taste
- 1/2 cup black beans, rinsed and drained
- 1/2 cup shredded cheddar cheese
- 1/4 cup diced red onion
- 1/4 cup sliced jalapeños
- 1/4 cup chopped cilantro
- Sour cream for serving (optional)

Instructions:

1. Preheat the oven to 400°F (200°C). Line a baking sheet with parchment paper.
2. Toss the sweet potato rounds in olive oil, salt, and pepper. Spread them out in a single layer on the baking sheet.
3. Bake for 15-20 minutes, flipping halfway through, until the sweet potatoes are crispy.
4. Remove from the oven and top with black beans, cheese, red onion, and jalapeños.
5. Return to the oven for 5-7 minutes, or until the cheese has melted.
6. Garnish with cilantro and serve with sour cream if desired.

Jalapeño Cheddar Cornbread Muffins

Ingredients:

- 1 1/2 cups cornmeal
- 1 cup all-purpose flour
- 1/4 cup sugar
- 1 tbsp baking powder
- 1/2 tsp salt
- 1/2 tsp garlic powder
- 1 cup buttermilk
- 2 large eggs
- 1/4 cup melted butter
- 1/2 cup shredded cheddar cheese
- 2 jalapeños, finely chopped
- 1 tbsp chopped green onions (optional)

Instructions:

1. Preheat the oven to 375°F (190°C). Grease a muffin tin or line it with paper liners.
2. In a large bowl, mix cornmeal, flour, sugar, baking powder, salt, and garlic powder.
3. In a separate bowl, whisk together buttermilk, eggs, and melted butter.
4. Stir the wet ingredients into the dry ingredients, then fold in the cheddar cheese, jalapeños, and green onions (if using).
5. Divide the batter evenly among the muffin cups, filling them about 2/3 full.
6. Bake for 18-20 minutes, or until a toothpick inserted into the center comes out clean.
7. Serve warm.

Mini Chicken and Waffle Bites

Ingredients:

- 12 mini frozen waffles, thawed and cut into quarters
- 12 small pieces of cooked, boneless chicken (fried or grilled)
- 1/4 cup maple syrup
- 1 tbsp Dijon mustard
- 1 tbsp melted butter
- Toothpicks for assembly

Instructions:

1. Toast the mini waffles according to package instructions and cut each waffle into quarters.
2. Arrange the waffle quarters on a serving platter.
3. Place a piece of chicken on top of each waffle.
4. In a small bowl, whisk together maple syrup, Dijon mustard, and melted butter.
5. Drizzle the syrup mixture over the chicken and waffle bites.
6. Secure each bite with a toothpick and serve warm.